Landscapes of Texas

Photographs from *Texas Highways* Magazine

Introduction by JOHN GRAVES

Preface by FRANKLIN T. LIVELY, BOB PARVIN,
and TOMMIE PINKARD

TEXAS A&M UNIVERSITY PRESS   College Station

Library of Congress Cataloging in Publication Data

Main entry under title:

Landscapes of Texas.

    (The Louise Lindsey Merrick Texas environment series;
no. 3)
    1. Texas—Description and travel—1951– —Views.
2. Natural history—Texas—Pictorial works.
I. Graves, John, 1920– II. Texas highways.
III. Series: Louise Lindsey Merrick Texas environment
series; no. 3.
F387.L36   976.4   79-5274
ISBN 0-89096-088-7

Manufactured in the United States of America

Sixth Printing

Dear Nancy,
"The Street" will not be
the same without you!
We've shared some unforgettable
laughs + memories — I won't forget
if you don't + I wish you weren't
leaving but wish you much happiness
in your new home. Take Care — or "Ah do not care"
Love,
Kathy

Dear Nancy,
what a pleasure
to know you and your
family. You are a very
talented woman. I'm
glad I have the little
And you cared and Nancy, although I haven't known
the pins. Home + good you very long. I'll miss
life. God bless you. you + wish you all
Love, the best in Florida.!!
Cecilia Anne

Nancy,
Best of Luck from
your favorite BUNCO
partner! I'll miss
you. Maybe I'll win
now!
Mary Campana

Nancy,
Best wishes to
all of you,
Juana Marie

Nancy,
Best wishes in
your new home.
wish you well in
Florida.
Vicki Gruis

Number Three: The Louise Lindsey Merrick Texas Environment Series

Landscapes of Texas

Contents

Preface

Many visitors come to Texas expecting to find a landscape of unremitting sand and cactus. As a matter of fact, Texas contains five of the seven major physiographic regions that exist within the borders of the United States. Only the Pacific highlands to the west and the Appalachian highlands to the east are not represented in the Lone Star state.

For some, Texas will be a winter vacationland of palm trees and sunny beaches. A visitor to the Panhandle will find endless vistas of windblown croplands. To others, Texas will offer desolate mountains that challenge the outdoorsman or mysterious caverns awaiting the dedicated spelunker. Still others will recall green hills and fat cattle, bluebonnets and red clover. It all depends upon which part of Texas you visit.

A variety of climates in Texas also contributes to the diversity of landscapes. About the only generalization anyone can make about the Texas climate is that it's mostly warm. Three of the four climatic regions in the state, all except the area at the top of the Panhandle, are "subtropical."

To the east is the humid subtropical area, with high temperatures, a long growing season, and enough rain to support vast forests. The average annual rainfall varies from about 56 inches at the Sabine River to about 30 at the western extension of the zone. By contrast, the subtropical desert region of West Texas has perhaps 8 inches of rain a year. Between these two areas, the subtropical steppe region sweeps from Brownsville on Texas' southern tip to Amarillo in the Panhandle and covers some three-fifths of the state along the way. Rainfall can be from 10 to 30 inches a year, and is, if you ask the farmers and ranchers, totally unreliable. Natural vegetation here means grass and shrub, compared with lush forests to the east and cactus and other desert plants to the west.

Only the Panhandle north of the Canadian River, part of a climatic region that extends all the way through the central United States and into Canada, has truly cold weather—and the shortest growing season in the state

(180 days). Average precipitation is nothing to brag about, either; it totals about 18 inches, including snow. Ranchers and wheat farmers here have been heard to mutter that there's nothing between their land and the North Pole except a barbed wire fence, and two strands are down.

Texas has more square miles—6,300—of inland waterways than any other state except Alaska. Included in the state's 23 million acres of woodlands are 11.2 million acres of commercial forests and four national forests with 664,049 acres. Ninety-one peaks in far West Texas tower more than a mile high. Texas has hundreds of miles of Gulf Coast beaches, all open to the public. Barrier islands stretching northward from the Rio Grande along almost the entire length of the coastline provide swimming, fishing, and boating for millions each year.

Invariably, a newcomer to Texas will ask, "Just how big is Texas?" You might get different answers from different sources, but according to the state's General Land Office, the area of Texas totals approximately 275,400 square miles, including submerged lands in the Gulf of Mexico. If you find this difficult to imagine, consider: one of every two hundred acres of the world's dry surface is in Texas. From east to west—from Orange to El Paso— Texas measures 773 miles. Between the northwest corner of the Panhandle and the mouth of the Rio Grande are 801 miles.

In that vast expanse, Texas has more urban areas than any other state, including thirteen cities with more than 100,000 population. Houston, with more than 1.6 million, is the nation's sixth largest city; Dallas ranks eighth and San Antonio tenth. Yet 80 percent of the state's area is devoted not to cities, but to farms and ranches. And Texas still has more cattle than people, about 14 million head at last count.

Other things a newcomer doesn't expect to find in Texas are the diverse crops. The state is one of the leading producers of rice, sugar beets, peanuts, sunflower seeds, and sugar cane. In 1978, Texas ranked first in acreage production of cabbage and spinach, and second in cantaloupes, carrots, bell peppers, onions, and watermelons. The sweetest and juiciest oranges in the world come from the Rio Grande Valley. And each winter the Valley supplies the nation with its best grapefruit—the Texas Ruby Red.

Because of its diverse geography, Texas has more native animals and birds than any other state. Three-fourths of all known American birds have been identified in Texas (540 species). No other state offers such a variety. Our strategic location on the North American continent acts as a funnel for migrating birds from as far away as South America. Wildlife refuges along the Gulf Coast and in the Rio Grande Valley support rare and endangered species, as well as large concentrations of familiar birds. The whooping crane makes his winter home in the Aransas National Wildlife Refuge on the coast.

One hundred forty-two species of animals, including some that are extremely rare, call Texas home. A critter most folks associate only with movies about the Amazon jungles thrives right here in Texas—the alligator. An estimated 60,000 of them, most of which are concentrated in the southeast corner of the state, can be found in rivers from the Rio Grande to the Sabine. Jefferson County alone contains about 20,000.

In the Big Thicket area of Southeast Texas, carnivorous pitcher plants trap unwary insects. Far to the west, rare red Mexican silenes hide in cool, secluded canyons. On Padre Island, morning glories proliferate across lonely dunes. Texas' 5,000 species of wild flowers, more than can be found in any other state, are an indication of the state's great diversity. Each spring bluebonnets, buttercups, Indian paintbrush, and other flowering plants spread their blossoms statewide, draping festive serapes over highway shoulders.

Eight hundred thousand acres of plantings line the 71,000 miles of Texas highways. With plows churning the earth each season and bulldozers clearing more land for shopping centers, the highway right-of-way may be the last bastion of wild flowers. Texas highway rights-of-way are the most undisturbed, yet protected and cared for, land in the state. In some areas, wild flowers that have entirely disappeared from farm and pasturelands now thrive in profusion along highway corridors. It's no accident. For fifty years specifications for highway construction have included precise requirements for preservation of native wild flowers, shrubs, and trees. Each spring an administrative order from the State Department of Highways and Public Transportation directs maintenance crews throughout the state not to mow until wild flowers have bloomed and their seeds matured.

Where a new highway is built, the topsoil is gathered and stockpiled.

When the new pavement is in place and broad shoulders have been shaped to their final contours, that topsoil, rich in leaf mold, humus, roots, and seed, is brought back and spread over the foundation earth. New seeds and plants are added, plus fertilizer blended for the particular locality. To ensure renewal of life, the highway contractor is required to implement a precise watering schedule. On steeper grades, tons of hay are bought, chopped, and spread as mulch to prevent erosion until native flora can secure the slopes. For those who drive the highways of Texas, the result is measured in beauty by the mile.

All the photographs in this book come from *Texas Highways* magazine, which since 1974 has had the responsibility for recording the history, scenery, people, and events within the state. *Texas Highways* goes back two more decades, to 1953. Even before that time it had a precursor entitled *Construction and Maintenance Bulletin*. The pre-1974 issues, however, were directed solely at department employees and were filled with articles on highway design, construction, and maintenance. In 1953, the magazine began a short feature each month about well-known Texas landmarks, historic sites, or state parks. Soon, other articles of general interest appeared. And *Texas Highways* began to encourage its readers to "discover Texas."

Tom H. Taylor, director of the Travel and Information Division where the magazine is published, believed that Texas needed a monthly supplement to other materials the division was producing for travelers. He wanted to develop a magazine that would display colorfully the heritage and culture, as well as the physical beauty, of Texas. Gradually, *Texas Highways* has achieved his goal. With a new format and color photographs, it has attracted readers outside the Highway Department.

The first issue addressed entirely to the general reader appeared in May, 1974. By April of the following year, the Texas legislature was impressed enough to pass a concurrent resolution naming *Texas Highways* the official state travel magazine and directing that "every effort be made to enlarge its growing family of readers." Encouraged, *Texas Highways* proceeded to let the world know about the beauties of the Lone Star state, the things to see and do here. Most important, the magazine introduced the state to its own citizens; about 90 percent of its growing subscription list remains Texas addresses.

The State Department of Highways and Public Transportation cannot, of course, take credit for all that beauty. The wild flowers were here, as were the mountains, the pine trees, and the grassy plains, long before man arrived on the scene. Yet today the department is helping to retain that image and to preserve the environment that made possible the pictures on the following pages.

Franklin T. Lively
Bob Parvin
Tommie Pinkard

Texas Highways

Introduction
Some Notes on Texas Landscapes
by JOHN GRAVES

Not very long ago I was taken for a jeep ride on a fine ranch not far from Abilene by its aging but vigorous owner, who lives on the place and operates it, as his ancestors did before him in times when it took two days to drive a wagon to the nearest town. Showing interested visitors around is something many ranchers like to do, for their daily and absorbing concern with their land, with animals and grass and water and fences and the rest, is a lonesome thing much of the time and they find it good occasionally to share it with someone else who's willing to listen and look and has a little comprehension of what he's seeing and hearing.

There had been generous rains that spring and early summer and the range was in prime condition, its grasses tall and still green even in late July. You could see very little bare ground and only a sprinkling of the mesquites that dog that belt of country, for it is a special sort of place that has been lovingly handled and seldom overgrazed since the 1880's when barbed wire, by doing away with the open range, made good management feasible. Which is not to say, of course, that fences per se led all ranchers into good range practices, but these had been special people....

We angled up out of a river canyon in the jeep and topped a rise and came down into the gentle valley of a creek, with willows and cottonwoods along it and on the solidly grassed slopes to either side fat white-faced mama cows and their rounded chunky calves. I said it was a pretty sight.

The rancher grinned. "Hell yes, it is," he said. "And you know what's the best thing of all about it?"

"What's that?"

"What's best about it," he said, "is that there's not a single thing here that's special enough to bring a tourist five miles out of his way. They just drive on by to the Big Bend or Mexico or somewhere else and let us live in peace."

This is true of much of our state, whether or not one views it as an advantage. What most of us natives would call "typical" Texas landscapes consist of prairies and plains, and these days they are not by and large a heavy attraction to travelers and photographers and others in quest of natural drama, except perhaps when wild flowers are in bloom. They are the basis of the state's farming and ranching and hence of its real and lasting natural wealth, and in the beginning they were dramatic enough—thickly grassed expanses extending from horizon to horizon under wide bright skies, sustaining with their richness uncountable swarms of wild creatures, drinking into their spongy dark soils such rainwater as fell, using it and filtering it and then feeding it out to clear, tree-shaded, fish-crowded streams that felt their way southeastward, with the land's vast gentle tilt, toward the estuarial bays of the Gulf Coast. Few literate travelers who saw the region in those virgin times failed to comment with a degree of awe on all that space and wealth of life, even if some among them, bred to the forests and dripping moisture of the older states to the east, were made uneasy by this open country's strangeness.

The grasslands, originally covering about three-quarters of what is now Texas, neither were nor are all alike but varied greatly in topography and ground cover. In some regions they were rolling and in others flat and still others quite rough, according to the dictates of millions of years of geological and climatic change. Some were savannah in type, with mottes of trees here and there, some bald of all but the grass itself, which very notably changed in aspect from east to west as average rainfall diminished, the horse-high bluestems and Indiangrass and switchgrass of the better-watered prairies giving way to a sod of shorter and shorter species in the west and finally to the spaced bunch grasses of semidesert places.

These lands' primeval beauty made up of limitless views and untouched wildness was foredoomed when white men showed up, for the plains and prairies were very usable, and therefore most parts of them were used hard as soon as the newcomers got a good toehold here. This began quite early in areas like the Rio Grande Plain reaching from south of San Antonio to the

Mexican border, where from Spanish days onward huge numbers of longhorned cattle roamed unfenced and slowly thinned or destroyed the grass so that thorny scrub took over, the huisache and cactus and catclaw and guajillo and mesquite and other hostile flora that today typify the region known to its Latins as the *brasada* and to Anglos as the Brush Country. It has its own tough rawhide charm both scenically and as the matrix of a lingering, hard, colorful human way of life, recorded in its prime and given resonance for reading Texans by the hand of its native son J. Frank Dobie. Its soils' fecundity still nurtures stout cattle and hordes of brush-loving wild things, or lush crops too where irrigation water can be had. But it isn't what it was to start with, nor will it ever be again. Brush these days can be held at bay with bulldozers and root plows and herbicides and the like, albeit expensively, but it creeps back in if neglected for a couple of years or so, and the wide-open self-perpetuating grasslands of early times there have vanished not to return.

So have they elsewhere, for the most part. In steeply up-and-down parts of the Edwards Plateau like the beloved Hill Country, as well as in other rough limestone regions such as the section of the northerly Grand Prairie where I live, the destruction of aboriginal grasses by overgrazing and haphazard frontier farming initiated a tremendous loss of soil built up under grass over thousands of years. Storm water sloshing downhill across bare ground picked up dirt as silt and raced with it toward the distant sea through a network of turbid creeks and rivers that no longer held swarming populations of fish but indeed, some of them, ceased to be true creeks and rivers and flowed only after big rains.

This soil loss, which took place in other parts of the state too just as it had taken place all around the Mediterranean and throughout much of Asia thousands of years before from similar causes, was somehow most dramatic in hilly limestone places where the soils, though good, had never been extremely deep above bedrock and were often washed away completely when the woven, retentive mat of grass roots and crowns was eaten or plowed off. Behind the house on our stock farm there is a hillside that supports a fair stand of the versatile introduced Asian grass known as King Ranch bluestem, but the grass however hardy and adaptable is never thick enough on the hill to hide entirely the white stones among which it grows or the rims of bedrock ledges protruding along the land's contours. Limestone is an omnipresent element of the landscape in our hills, speckling any vista with pale dots and patches and streaks, inhibiting grass and productivity, ruling everywhere except in small flat creekbottom fields with still enough earth in them for crops, seeming to have belonged eternally just where it is now.

But it didn't belong here historically, at least not out in the open for everyone to see. It is the land's skeleton, and skeletons are supposed to be hidden. Old men now dead have told me that this hillside behind my house was once part of a cottonfield until it "wore out," before which of course it had had heavy grazing as a segment of the open range, and in those uses hung its destiny. Sometimes when I study it, as one does study a piece of ground close by, I indulge myself in a little fantasy of standing on a certain shelf of ledgerock and then being transported back in time. Ten or twelve years ago I would have been standing on the same shelf among thick cedar and oak, bulldozed off since then to give the grass a chance. As my fantasy machine ticks retrogressively to eighty or ninety years back, I find myself in the old ones' sloping deadly cottonfield, up to my knees or so in bare-plowed, rain-grooved, rather tired soil. But at a hundred and fifty, in full virgin times, if my feet are still on that ledge most or all of the rest of me is encased in magnificent dark prairie dirt topped with solid tall grass. There is no telling at this point whether the land's surface would reach to my waist or my chest or my ears or over my head, for no records hold that sort of data for these unnoteworthy hills. What is certain is that the subtraction was immense, and fairly quick, and permanent.

In these rough limestone areas the brush that moved in to cover the land's shamed nudity—our equivalent of the *brasada*'s thorny thickets—was hardwood scrub and the juniper all Texans call cedar, good for fenceposts but not much else. Goats and sheep do well enough here if their owners can keep coyotes and other epicurean varmints in check, but cattle need much continuing help from bulldozers and exotic grasses and supplemental feed, along with close attention to the avoidance of overstocking and new ruin.

In the near portion of West Texas where my ranching friend lives undisturbed by sightseers—the mainly red-soiled Rolling Prairies (sometimes called the Red Rolling Plains and sometimes other things, these nomenclatural usages being apparently negotiable)—the invasive scrub is thirsty mesquite, cursed and battled throughout millions of acres of what was once prime ranchland and often still is, if the brush can be controlled and the grass restored and kept in place. All these forms of brush in the old grasslands derive from the fact that nature abhors not only vacuums but barenesses; where man manages to obliterate one form of cloaking vegetation she usually answers him by providing another, and if he finds too hard a use for that one also—as Greeks and Levantines for instance did with goats and sheep that ate off the invading brush itself as well as any grass that came back—she tries perhaps another time or two before giving up and letting the whole thing turn to pure desert or bare rock, an ultimate and irreversible transition that can be observed in progress in many dry parts of the world today, including some of our own.

Of the other Texas grasslands, or what were once grasslands, most escaped the worst effects of heavy use through their relative flatness, which slowed the sweep of storm waters and held erosion down. Because of this flatness also, much of their surface is cropland now, often still highly productive because of modern techniques of tillage and fertilization that appeared on the scene before exhaustion was complete. The damp prairies along the upper coast are thus. So are the gentler sections of the fabled Blacklands that stretch from near San Antonio to Oklahoma and beyond, and the level High Plains that top the Cap Rock, where intensive farming came late and only through exploitation of vast underground reserves of water for irrigation, a resource that is dwindling now from enormously heavy pumping during the past three or four prosperous decades.

Thus the plains and prairies, those most characteristic landscapes that are inside all of us who think of ourselves as Texans, whether or not we inhabit them. Out of their primeval extensiveness and fertility were formed not only a dynamic ranching economy whose mores good and bad still serve as reference points for even urban people, but also indeed the American cowboy himself and the West's cattle culture as the world at large knows and treasures them. If such lands are not too picturesque these days, the fact remains that from their qualities—from the very process of their rape, for that matter—legends and history and ways of life were built. Texas, says an old verse, grew from hide and horn; hide and horn in their turn grew from prairie grass.

The "scenery" of which Texas can now boast, the sort of natural sites and areas that people don't just drive by on their way to Mexico or somewhere but make a detour or a trip to view, lies for the most part either in regions distinct from the old grasslands, or along those grasslands' fringes, or in transition zones between them. The Hill Country crescent of the Edwards Plateau, for instance, sits behind the Balcones Escarpment curving down from Austin to Del Rio and constituting the plateau's eastern and southern edge, sharply marking its separation from the Blackland prairies and the Rio Grande Plain. Once mainly rough grassy savannah themselves, the hills are dark now with the cedar and oak that took over when the grass was gone, and loom in some reaches hundreds of feet above the lowlands they confront, not everywhere dramatically but always as a solid impressive line of change. With their thousands of secret valleys and views and their lacework of cypress-bordered watercourses fed by the deep cold springs that are a special blessing of geological fault zones, they have served generations of flatlanders as a place to fish and hunt and pleasantly loaf. On the whole this has been beneficial to the natives through the money it brings in, since most of them during this century have found agriculture and animal husbandry to be a fairly tough go, for reasons revealed by that time machine I have fantasized. Their topsoil went the same steep route as mine, and much of their subsoil too.

The Cap Rock escarpment wavering north-south along the Panhandle's axis, where the flat High Plains abruptly fall away to red country that is the western limit of the Rolling Prairies, is a more striking zone of change if less hospitable in its crannies. Scalloped with startling age-gnawed canyons like the Palo Duro that once served wintering Indians as a refuge against winter's northwesterly blasts (and served them also as a trap when Mackenzie's troopers caught them there), the escarpment displays a cross section of the sediments that underlie the Plains, a debris apron laid down anciently by unbelievable rivers coursing down out of the Rockies when those mountains were young and immensely high. Its ruggedness is also a vast relief to the eye after a day spent driving across either plains or prairies, and must have been even more so in the old wagon and horseback days when the time involved was weeks.

To people who care about country and the way it works, some of the other grassland transition areas have interest too, even when unspectacular. Such are the East and West Cross Timbers, two strange fingers of post-oak forest, mostly scrub growth or sandy cropland now, that poke down into the central part of the state from the Red River and divide the Blacklands from the Grand Prairie and the Grand Prairie from the Rolling Prairies. Going west, they are the last real timber, except in riverbottoms, that you find before the mountains beyond the Pecos. In frontier times they marked pretty well the limit of feasibility for log cabins and other forest institutions that the early settlers had brought with them, and hence were a sort of jumping-off place into a purely Western way of life. Frontiersmen knew well also such occasional physiographic surprises as the Llano Uplift or Central Mineral Zone, that queer circular region of pink granite and marble and other igneous or metamorphic stuff surrounded by unrelieved sedimentary limestone, and the Monahans Sands, a hundred-mile strip of isolated dune country straddling the state boundary where New Mexico corners in at the base of the Texas Panhandle.

Texas itself being a sort of wide transition zone where historically Easterners learned to be Westerners because of diminishing rainfall and the petering out of forests, it is not very unexpected to observe that at the eastern and western extremes of the state lie two large regions that seem to have little in common with the rest of it and nothing at all in common with each other. These are the East Texas woods and the country beyond the Pecos River. The one is an Old Southern enclave with heavy black populations, heavier rainfall, pine and hardwood forests, and ways of speaking and doing things more akin to those of Alabama than to those of, say, Brady or San Saba. The other belongs to the mountain West of deserts and high plateaus and stark ranges and canyons and sparse settlement. Both have grasslands of their own islanded in desert or forest; indeed the East has more than it had in the beginning, for during the past few decades old farmed-out croplands there have increasingly been sowed to improved strains of exotic grass and used for raising beef, so that in those parts, so to speak, the West has moved itself eastward, high-heeled boots and all.

But essentially East Texas is immemorial mixed Southern tall forest, typified most purely in what is left of the Big Thicket of the southeastern flats, where until lately the swamps and the sheer density of growth inhibited the heavy logging that wiped out big trees in most of the rest of the region in the nineteenth and early twentieth centuries. And essentially the Trans-Pecos is dry rough desert despite irrigated farming here and there and fine ranch country in places like the Stockton Plateau around Alpine. Its flavor is epitomized for most of us in the Big Bend National Park, where visitors from all over come to wonder at the horrific but handsome evidence of nature's upheavals and enduring dry harshness, most Texans feeling as alien there as the folks from anywhere else.

People of course are a part of most landscapes too by now, people and the things they have built or destroyed or changed or brought in or thrown away. In the Old World their venerable traces and constructions frequently add meaning and what is generally called charm to a countryside, laying out history's implications for the beholder as in a painting. Over here the charm is more often scant or lacking, but if we haven't been on deck for a long time as time goes we have been here very busily, and in a place like Texas, used hard in most parts for at least a hundred years now and in some sections for as much as two hundred, there is no ignoring man and his works historic or otherwise. Nor, I guess, would most of us want to. Even the beer-joint and junkyard strips along the approaches to Texas cities are integrally a part of the way we are now, just as oil fields are, and the cogent memory of the vanished pristine grasslands. What men have done here in the past and what they are doing now, whether good or bad in absolute terms if absolute terms are definable, do make up our own history and shape us still. Agriculture, ranching, the spread of towns, petroleum, dams and their reservoirs, manufacturing, mining, lumbering, power generation, ethnic migrations and frictions and blendings—all these and a good many other human activities and effects have exercised stout impact not only on physical Texas but on our conception of it. And more often than not they are tied in with the land and its quirks and possibilities, as well as with the sort of people who came here in the first place.

Regard, for example, the goodly dollop of Old World charm that we find in the stone fences and houses and barns and neat villages of certain parts of the Hill Country such as the area around Fredericksburg. In part these testify to a historic blunder on the part of the philanthropic Society for the Protection of German Immigrants in Texas, an old-country outfit which brought several thousand settlers to the region in the mistaken belief that it was prime agricultural terrain like the coastal prairie between the Brazos and the Colorado, where earlier Teutons had set up holdings, prospered, and written glowing letters home to make Texas a byword north of the Rhine. But mainly those well-managed and pretty and orderly hill farmsteads and towns are a testament to the tenacity and cultural strength of the Germans who came and stuck and made the best of what they found, including limestone rocks and Comanches.

And consider the dry, high South Plains, the Llano Estacado of the Spaniards where short grass and space and the wild cattle called buffalo seemed unlimited not very long ago. Its tradition of ranching empires built after the extermination of the Indians and the buffalo and its present agricultural splendor manifested in verdant squares of cotton and wheat and milo and corn and sugarbeets and whatnot covering league after league of level land, broken only by the grain elevators and water towers of thriving towns, have both been possible only because of a secret the land possessed, the Ogallala aquifer, a vast thick formation full of what some have called "fossil water" accumulated through ages past, tapped but lightly by the cattlemen's indispensable windmills, but being depleted these days, as we have noted, at a fierce rate, so that more history is likely to be made within a few years by its decline to inutility.

Suppose Spaniards and Mexicans had not been held almost immobile for a century or so at their bases in San Antonio and Santa Fe by the truculent Comanches and thus prevented from spreading out as they were culturally prepared to do, with their missions and presidios and flat-roofed towns and haciendas, onto the western ranges and up the Great Plains' sweep. What in that case would have been the aspect and flavor of our state and other regions beyond its bounds? Suppose the Anglo-Americans who settled big parts of the Blacklands had not been Southern and cotton-minded, had not set up a briefly booming plantation way of life and agriculture there whose evidence lingers down in pleasant gingerbread towns like Waxahachie. (And, intriguingly, in census figures that show notable black populations as far as a line of counties marking the western limit of those Blacklands but no farther; soils and rainfall beyond that line were not friendly to plantation ways, nor did main settlement of the westerly regions come during times of slavery.) And consider why so many Blackland courthouses are ornate costly Victorian affairs in contrast with smaller and simpler ones found in the seats of many gravelly, less fertile counties of the Post Oak Belt to the east, and whether the nearly tropical lower Rio Grande Valley, once mainly an impenetrable thorny tangle along the river where white-winged doves and chachalacas and ocelots and such lived unannoyed except by one another, would have attracted canny Midwestern immigrants and prospered as greenly as it has if the rest of the nation had not been direly short of places where citrus and fresh winter vegetables could be grown. Or what a town like Desdemona, née Hogtown, with its sleepy air and its yawning empty buildings, would have looked like if its oil pool had only held out. . . .

People impose themselves on land and the land imposes itself on them; ways of living and building and farming come in with settlers and then evolve into other ways in accordance not only with the ethos the people have brought and what happens to them there, but also with the land's possibilities and demands. Thus landscapes where man's presence past and current is seen do have historic weight in Texas quite as certainly as in Tuscany or Scotland or along the castled Loire. Most of us Texans so far have been too absorbed with acting and doing and making meanings to have worried much about what those meanings are and to have read their lessons, but that doesn't keep them from being all around us when we look. Some are proud meanings and others less so; some are simple and clear and others need ferreting out; some affirm Manifest Destiny while others prophesy exhaustion and deserts and doom. But all have a part in the wide, varied, rather improbable place we call Texas, and have a part in us too, insofar as we are Texans.

Plates

East Texas

This part of Texas will ambush the senses of all who enter it with preconceptions of sand and cacti around every bend. It has a style that does not fit the boots-and-saddle image of big sky country. Instead, White Oak Bayou, Caddo Lake, and lazy waterways like the Trinity, Neches, and Sabine rivers are shadowed by forests that still cover more than twenty million acres—the western border of the great southern piney woods. It also is the domain of the Big Thicket, with its incredible varieties of flora, where orchids bloom in the shadow of prickly pears, and cypress swamps are separated from longleaf pines by only a few steps through a blanket of mushrooms.

Here one's vision narrows to the breadth of wooded corridors. Sweet-scented lanes retain the savor of the Deep South and antebellum cotton culture. It is an "old home" place where easy living is a steadfast tradition.

But there are other dimensions to this green-belted land. It is a refreshing mixture of the old and new, where the latest oil and lumber technology coexists with yeoman activities of a bygone era.

Pitcher plant, Big Thicket

Backpackers, Angelina National Forest

Opposite: Dogwood blossoms, Big Thicket near Palestine

Bouton Lake, Angelina National Forest

Opposite: Nature trail in Davy Crockett National Forest

Lake Hawkins, Wood County

Bluebonnets in pine forest, Daingerfield State Park

Opposite: Bluebonnets near College Station

Palmettos and towering hardwoods near Saratoga in the Big Thicket

Gaillardia lanceolata

White daisies

Caddo Lake, Northeast Texas

Mixed hardwood forest near Caddo Lake

Overleaf: Fall-blooming wild flowers at Toledo Bend Reservoir

Caddo Lake, Northeast Texas

Trailing phlox

Wild azalea

Trillium

Cinnamon ferns in the Big
Thicket south of Woodville

Cinnamon fern

Bladderwort

Pitcher plants

Butterwort

Sundew

39

Tyler State Park, Northeast Texas

Coral root orchid, Big Thicket

Butterwort

Bladderwort

Fragrant water lily

Opposite: Dogwood, Gus Engling Wildlife Refuge near Palestine

Coral honeysuckle on pine tree

Opposite: Golden ragwort, south of Palestine

Texas Gulf Coast

As the gull flies, Texas' margin with the Gulf of Mexico extends for some 625 miles from the Sabine estuary to the mouth of the Rio Grande. But if every curve and cove along the way is tallied, there is nearly four times that amount of actual shoreline.

It is a shoreline of differences, with industrial Port Arthur as much a part of the coastal scene as the resorts at Port Isabel. Commercial fishermen and sportsmen annually share the teeming estuarine resources of the Gulf's bays and inlets with millions of migratory waterfowl, including a handful of whooping cranes.

For creatures of the air and water, the Texas Gulf Coast is a refuge for survival, a place of solitude and sanctuary. For humankind it has various attractions. It is the source of livelihood for some. Many more find it a recreational paradise for boating, fishing, surfing, and beachcombing. In the mesmeric pulse of waves along the beach, in the perfume of tropical winds, in the sunlight and everchanging cloud patterns there are refreshment and renewal.

Beached shrimp boat on South Padre Island

46

Sabine Pass Lighthouse

Old buoy on South Padre Island beach

Opposite: Galveston beach

Padre Island

Opposite: South Padre Island

Beachcombers on Padre Island

Opposite: Sandhill cranes

Avocet

Gadwalls

Whooping cranes

Birds flock at Aransas National Wildlife Refuge

Docks near Rockport

Marshlands near Sea Rim State Park

Intracoastal Waterway, Aransas
National Wildlife Refuge

54

Live-oak grove near Rockport

Clear Creek Channel on Galveston Bay

Corpus Christi's pleasure boat piers

Padre Island sand dunes

Harbor at Rockport

Shrimp boat harbor

57

Lettuce field in the Lower Rio Grande Valley

Marine Academy campus, Harlingen

Opposite: Palm trees and orchards in Rio Grande Valley

West Texas

The terrain of western Texas is often described as a kind of geological scrapyard. Such a jumble of forms and dimensions is contained in this land that the analogy seems fair. But no description easily fits its astonishing contrasts.

Many zones converge here. Just as the shadows of mountains seem to melt into the waves of heat in a mirage, so do the farthest extensions of the Rockies and Mexican deserts blend together in West Texas. The high rims of the Chisos, Davis, Guadalupe, and more than a dozen other ranges rise abruptly in the sandy wastes that reach north from Chihuahua. Across the region, ninety-one peaks, among them the highest in Texas, thrust more than a mile into the incandescent atmosphere. Biological perimeters overlap in fields of geological transition. Climates crisscross, lifeways commingle. And now, as he has forever, man treads here tentatively.

Life is based on extremes, isolation, and insufficiency. That plants or animals exist at all in many sun-scalded reaches is a lesson in ingenuity and will. That they flourish unexpectedly in other areas is an object of marvel.

Near the Chisos Mountains, Big Bend National Park

Mesas along the Rio Grande near Lajitas

Ancient Indian rock shelter at Lake Amistad

Opposite: Lake Amistad near Del Rio

The Window, Big Bend National Park

Overleaf: McKittrick Canyon, Guadalupe Mountains National Park

Rock study from the Big Bend country

Little settlement near Candelaria

Big Bend country

Overleaf: South Rim Trail in the Chisos Mountains

Black Gap Wildlife Management Area, Brewster County

The Chisos Basin, Big Bend National Park

Opposite: Aguja Creek, north of Fort Davis

Limestone bluffs on Devil's River

Fisherman on Devil's River

Opposite: Santa Elena Canyon, Big Bend National Park

75

Variegated canyons near Big Bend National Park

Layers of ash interbedded with sanidine crystals in Presidio County

Opposite: Tower in Big Bend badlands

Rock lettuce

Cory-cactus

Texas madrone tree

Opposite: Engelmann prickly pear and cholla cactus

El Camino del Rio and Bofecillos Mountains on the Rio Grande

Rich valleys upriver from Bofecillos Mountains

Opposite: Bofecillos Mountains overlooking the Rio Grande near Lajitas

Overleaf: Indian lodge, Davis Mountains State Park

Grazing land near Fort Davis

Overleaf: The 06 Ranch on the slopes of the Davis Mountains

Cattle graze over a mile high in the Davis Mountains

Roundup time on the 06 Ranch

Horse remuda for 06 roundup

Horses on the 06 Ranch

McKittrick Canyon

Indian Cliffs Ranch trail, east of El Paso

Opposite: Spanish dagger, Big Bend country

Cholla cactus

Hedgehog cactus

Eagle's claw (devil's head) cactus

Opposite: Rounding up horses on the 06 Ranch

Rain-filled waterholes in Hueco Tanks State Park

Rappellers on north mountain in Hueco
Tanks State Park

Park ranger in Hueco Tanks State Park

Opposite: Hueco Tanks State Park, east of El Paso

Wild flowers near syenite rock pile in Hueco Tanks State Park

Hueco Mountains near park

Opposite: Wild flowers near Hueco Tanks State Park

Agave

Muhly grass

Mixed forest and vegetation in Guadalupe
Mountains National Park

McKittrick Canyon

El Capitan Peak, Guadalupe Mountains

Opposite: Hikers in Guadalupe Mountains National Park

Opposite and above: Sand dunes, Monahans Sandhills State Park

Overleaf: Wild grass in Monahans Sandhills State Park

Panhandle Plains

Within the Panhandle's boundaries lie some of the flattest surfaces on earth. It is a place of everlasting horizons—naked to the elements, scourged by sun and wind, and possessed of monotony and sameness. Yet it also is a terrain of surprise and wonder. Blanco and Yellow House canyons, the incomparable Palo Duro, and the Cap Rock give vertical dimensions to an otherwise horizontal landscape. And the temper of its climate gives the country a constantly changing character. Sudden storms are exciting constituents of a life where demands are high and rewards uncertain.

This is a new land, made habitable for modern man only within the memory of some still living. Long the domain of livestock herds, much of the countryside is now watered from underground sources, and fields of wheat, cotton, and sorghum stretch out, it seems, forever. It is a place of harsh beauty where the sun's coming and going often is spectacular and where the simple change of season has a force unmatched in softer environs. The greening of spring and the alchemy of fall are special events that briefly transform both flatlands and canyons into glowing tapestries of color.

A storm sweeps the plains near Amarillo

Cottonwoods in Palo Duro Canyon

Lubbock Gardens

Prairie Dog Town Fork of Red River

Cattle on Panhandle ranch

Cottonwood canopy in a Palo Duro picnic area

Sandy lane near Canadian in the eastern Panhandle

110

Golden cottonwoods on Panhandle ranch headquarters near Amarillo

Overleaf: Palo Duro Canyon

Palo Duro's "Spanish Skirts"

Roundup time on the Coldwater Ranch, north of Amarillo

Opposite: Tule Canyon, southeast of Amarillo

Pioneer Village, near Canyon

Photographing a snow-glazed setting
Palo Duro Canyon

Dry bed of Canadian River

Opposite: January on Palo Duro Creek

117

Storm front near Dalhart

Above and opposite: Blue norther

Spring lightning in night sky over Canadian

Panhandle wheat field

Palo Duro Canyon reaches into the level plains

Opposite: Lake Meredith, north of Amarillo

Central Texas

That part of Texas extending north from Austin to Fort Worth and Dallas and south as far as San Antonio is a region that has taken kindly to man's presence. Whether blackland prairies or limestone hills, the countryside first attracted immigrants from around the world and more recently native Americans seeking their fortune in the "sun belt." And despite urban encroachments upon an environment that until a few decades ago was predominantly rural, it remains a place of promise and hope for those residing here.

Spring is its premier season, when the bluebonnets flourish along every roadside in concert with a myriad other floral offerings. Then too is when the region's rivers, the Trinity and Brazos, the Guadalupe and the Colorado, flow sweetest.

Nor are all the natural attractions above ground. For those inclined to do so, there are numerous caves, grottoes, and "sinkholes" to explore around San Marcos and elsewhere in the Hill Country.

Hill Country bluebonnets

Sheep grazing near the Guadalupe River

Cattle on the LBJ Ranch near Stonewall

Frio River at Horse Collar Bluff

Chinaberry beside an abandoned farm-house near Canyon Lake

Fall color in the Hill Country

Maples in Sabinal Canyon

Opposite: Sweetgums and pines

Maximilian sunflower

Gay feather and goldenrod

Wild aster

Black-eyed susans near outcropping of Hill Country granite

Rainbow cactus

Yellow and white daisies,
Burnet County

Prickly-pear blossoms

Maidenhair fern in limestone outcroppings of creek in Sabinal Canyon

Pond in Sabinal Canyon

Maple grove on creek in Sabinal Canyon

Maple leaves among fern   Cypress trees along the Sabinal River near Utopia

Sabinal River opens wide into valley below Sabinal Canyon

Boaters on Comal River in Landa Park, New Braunfels

John Frederick Sauer home in LBJ Park

Opposite: Bluebonnets and yucca in Central Texas

Lost Maples State Park in Sabinal Canyon

Opposite: Lost pines in Bastrop State Park

Spring rainstorm, near San Marcos

Enchanted Rock, north of Fredericksburg

Sandy Creek, near Enchanted Rock

Opposite: Prickly pear near the foot of Enchanted Rock

140

Eroded and collapsed bedrock surrounds Hamilton Pool

Maidenhair fern

Leaves and sticks layered with calcium

West Cave Preserve

Opposite: Elaborate draperies of travertine and dripstone

Spanish oak on hillside in autumn

Fall color on Sabinal River, Lost Maples State Park

Opposite: Spring water rushes over limestone bedrock in the Hill Country

Bluebonnets

Leather flower

Rain lilies, Inks Lake

Yucca

Indian paintbrush

Wild phlox

Opposite: Pink evening primrose and prickly pear, near Elgin

A back road in Coryell County, south of Gatesville

Old barn and windmill, east of Gatesville

Indian blanket (firewheel or gaillardia)

Maximilian sunflower

Redbud tree blossoms

Fruit-tree blossoms beside Town Lake in Austin

Wild flowers and oak tree on Mason County ranch

Winter on Turtle Creek in Dallas

Ice forms on cactus

Ice-glazed yaupon

155

Photographic Credits